Writers Who Inspired the World

Written by Roberta Stathis and Gregory Blanch

Brea, California

Writers Who Inspired the World

SERIES EDITOR: HEERA KANG
PROJECT EDITOR: ALLISON MANGRUM
ART DIRECTOR: LILIANA CARTELLI
ILLUSTRATOR: GINA CAPALDI
EDITORIAL CONSULTANTS: PATRICE GOTSCH, JILL KINKADE
EDITORIAL STAFF: KRISTIN BELSHER, SEAN O'BRIEN, CHRISTINE HOOD
SENIOR DESKTOP PUBLISHING COORDINATOR: KATHLEEN STYFFE
PRINTING COORDINATOR: CATHY SANCHEZ

An IDEA® Book by Ballard & Tighe, Publishers
P.O. Box 219, Brea, CA 92822-0219

Copyright ©2004 Ballard & Tighe, Publishers, a division of Educational IDEAS, Inc.

All rights reserved. No part of this publication may be reproduced in whole or in part or stored in a retrieval system, or transmitted in any form or by any means, electronic or mechanical, including photocopy, recording, or otherwise, without permission in writing from the publisher.

First Printing
ISBN 1-55501-591-3   Catalog #2-751

Contents

Introduction 4

Time Line 6

Lady Murasaki Shikibu 8

Dante Aligheri 18

Leo Africanus 26

Bartolomé de las Casas 34

Miguel Cervantes 40

William Shakespeare 48

Voltaire 60

Activities 70

Test Your Knowledge! 73

Glossary/Parts of Speech Key 74

Vowel Pronunciation Key 75

Index 76

Skills Index/Credits 77

Find Out More! 78

Acknowledgments 79

Introduction

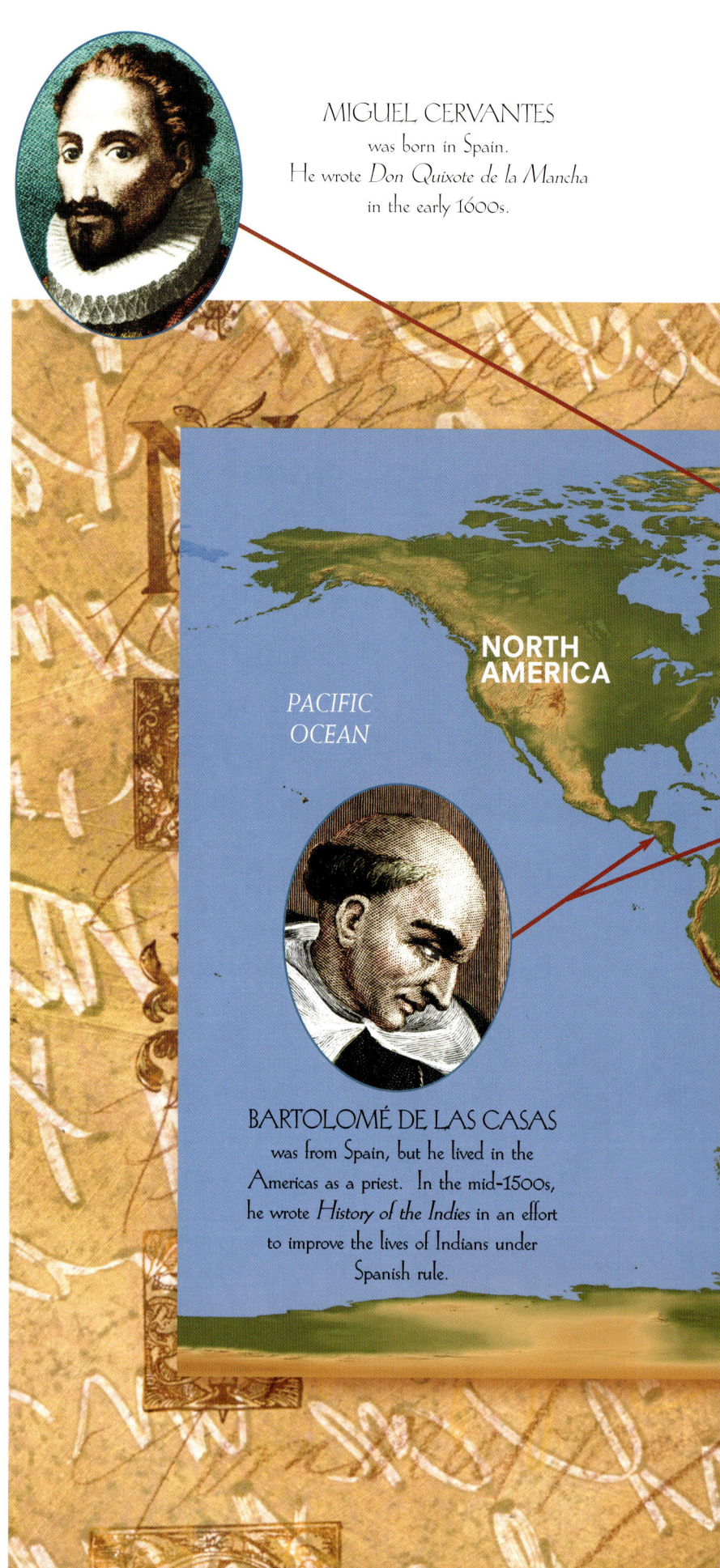

MIGUEL CERVANTES was born in Spain. He wrote *Don Quixote de la Mancha* in the early 1600s.

BARTOLOMÉ DE LAS CASAS was from Spain, but he lived in the Americas as a priest. In the mid-1500s, he wrote *History of the Indies* in an effort to improve the lives of Indians under Spanish rule.

Throughout history, people have used the written word to describe events, express emotions, influence opinions, and free the imaginations of their readers. Some writers have recorded facts and opinions that shape the way we think. Other writers have composed poetry, stories, and plays that affect the way we feel.

Inside these pages are the stories of just a few of the world's talented and influential writers who lived from the late 900s to the late 1700s. The writers in this book come from all over the world, and their words have influenced generations of readers. Each story includes details about the writer's life as well as a sampling of the writer's work.

Writers Who Inspired the World will take you on a journey through time and space. You will learn about writers whose works entertain, enlighten, and above all inspire.

Time Line

Having a common system to date events helps us compare events occurring at the same time in different parts of the world. Many experts in the Western world use the B.C./A.D. dating system. This system dates events from the birth of Jesus Christ, the central figure in the Christian religion. Events that took place before his birth are referred to as "before Christ" or B.C. dates. Traditionally, the term B.C. begins to be used around the time when human beings began to lead a more settled life, about 11,000 years ago. A.D. stands for the Latin words *anno Domini*, which means "in the year of our Lord." A.D. dates are given to events that occurred after Jesus's birth. A growing number of historians, archaeologists, and other academics also use the terms B.C.E. and C.E. to refer to these same periods of time. B.C.E. stands for "before Christian era" or "before common era." C.E. refers to "Christian era" or "common era." Some academic experts even use the term B.P., which stands for "before present." When we are not exactly sure of the date of an event, we use the Latin word *circa* which means "about." *Circa* is abbreviated c.

A.D. 1000

c. 1002 — Historians believe Lady Murasaki Shikibu finishes *The Tale of Genji*

c. 1307 — Dante begins writing *The Divine Comedy*

1500s — Leo Africanus travels throughout West Africa

TIPS on Reading a Time Line

Find the beginning and end dates.
Look at the far left and far right sides of the time line. These dates show you the range of time you are focusing on. What is the range of time for this book?

Check if the time line includes both B.C. and A.D. dates.
This book focuses on A.D. dates. When you read a time line with B.C. dates, remember that starting from the left, the B.C. dates become lower until the "0." After that, the A.D. dates go higher.

Think of other events that happened around the same time.
In the time line below, you can see that Shakespeare and Cervantes were writing around A.D. 1600. However, they did not write about the same things. As you read about these writers, think about how their experiences were the same and different.

Jump in!
Copy the time line onto a sheet of paper, but make the end date on the far right side extend to the present day. Insert yourself into the time line to see how long ago the events in this book happened. You also can include other important dates you have learned about.

- 1552 — Bartolomé de las Casas writes "In Defense of the Indians"
- c. 1600 — Leo Africanus's *The History and Description of Africa* is published
- c. 1595 — Shakespeare writes *Romeo and Juliet*
- c. 1605-1616 — Cervantes writes *Don Quixote de la Mancha*
- 1758 — Voltaire writes *Candide*

A.D. 1800

Lady Murasaki Shikibu

The Heian period—the time in Japanese history from about 794 to 1185—is often considered one of the most interesting periods in Japanese history. During this time, the Japanese aristocracy, or nobility, had the most influence in society—even more than the emperor! The aristocracy lived in the city of Kyoto and created a polite and refined culture that continues to influence Japanese culture today. The diaries, poetry, and other writings of Japanese nobles give us detailed information about the daily lives of the upper classes. During the Heian period, the woman we call Lady Murasaki Shikibu wrote the world's first novel, *The Tale of Genji*.

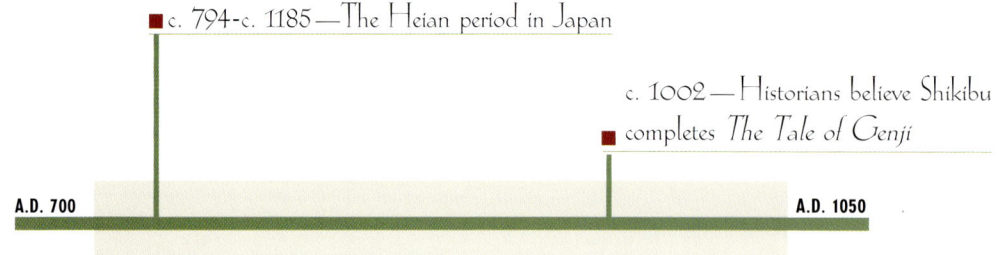

Lady Murasaki Shikibu wrote the world's first novel. A novel is a book of fiction—a story that comes from the writer's imagination. A novel is told by the actions, words, and thoughts of the characters in the story.

Fast Facts

NAME: Known to historians as Lady Murasaki Shikibu
BORN: c. 973-c. 978 in Japan
DIED: c. 1016-c. 1026 in Japan
FAMOUS WORK: The world's first novel, *The Tale of Genji*

attendant: a person who waits on or helps another

calligraphy: the art of fine handwriting

etiquette: a code of behavior and courtesy

An Intelligent Girl

Murasaki Shikibu was born between 973 and 978. Her real name is not known. The name Murasaki Shikibu is made up of two parts: "Shikibu" is the office her father held, and "Murasaki" is a character in her book. We know that Murasaki Shikibu's father was a minor government official and a scholar of Chinese language and literature. We also know that he hired a tutor to teach his son Chinese literature, **calligraphy**, and **etiquette**. At the time, it was not considered proper for women to learn these subjects. However, Murasaki Shikibu's father allowed her to attend the lessons unofficially. She appears to have been a better student than her brother. She wrote in her diary that she helped her brother "whenever he got stuck." On these occasions, her father could only sigh and say, "If only you were a boy, how proud and happy I should be." Some historians believe that Murasaki gained so much knowledge that later in life she had to hide much of what she knew.

Marriage and Court Life

Murasaki Shikibu married when she was in her late teens, and it appears that her marriage was happy. She and her husband had one daughter. However, in 1001, just a few years after their marriage, Murasaki Shikibu's husband died. Her father then arranged for her to become an **attendant** to the 16-year-old Empress Akiko.

Most historians agree that Lady Murasaki had begun writing *The Tale of Genji* by the time she entered the royal court. Many believe she finished writing this book around 1002.

Murasaki Shikibu wrote about the things she observed at the royal court. For example, she described how others dressed and how they behaved. She kept track of stories about the various court festivals, parties, and other activities. She described people's feelings and showed an interest in knowing why people acted the way they did. Scholars disagree about exactly when Lady Murasaki started writing *The Tale of Genji*, how long it took her to write it, and when she finished. However, everyone agrees that the story of Genji, the shining prince, is a wonderful tale filled with vivid details about court life in Japan during this time.

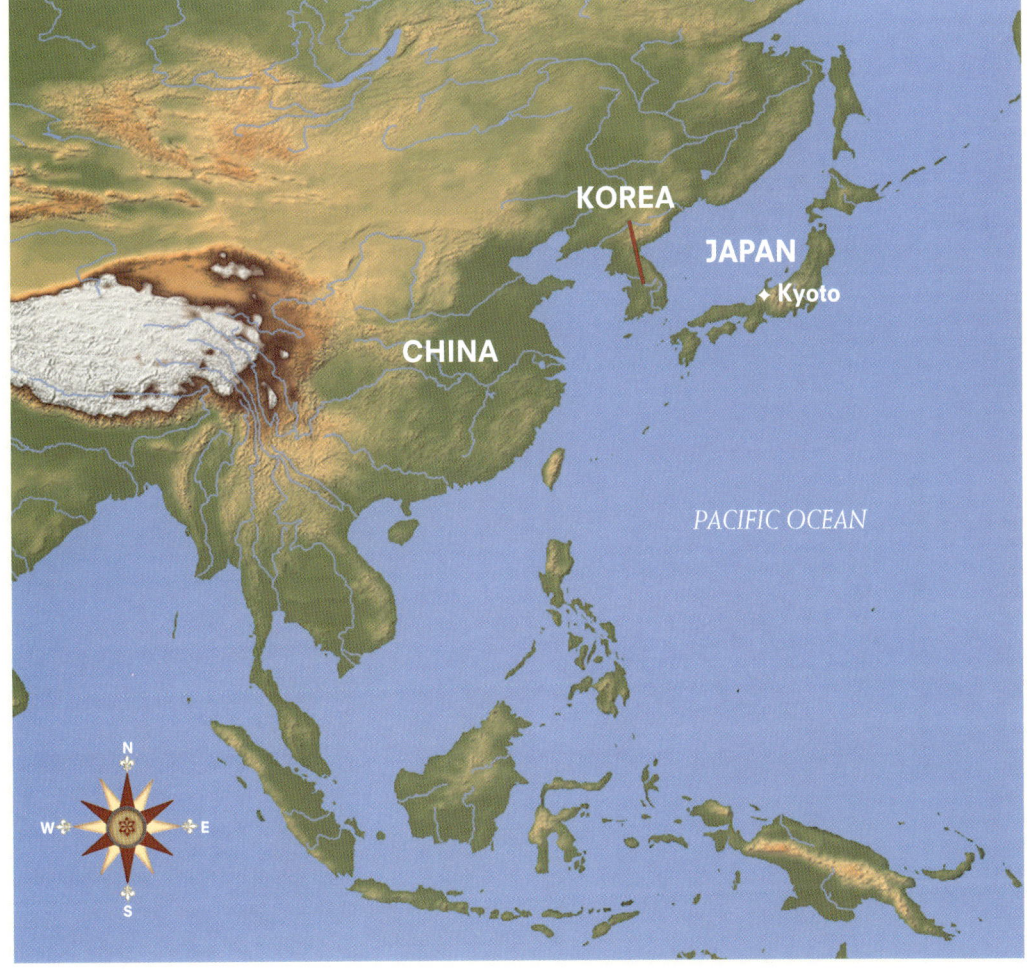

Lady Murasaki Shikibu was born in Japan during the Heian period.

concubine: a woman who lives with and is supported by a man, but who is not his wife; mistress

The Tale of Genji

The Tale of Genji tells the story of a prince named Genji. Genji's father is an emperor and his mother is the emperor's favorite **concubine**. To protect his son, the emperor makes the boy a member of the "Genji" clan. This meant that the boy was a member of the aristocracy, but it also meant that Genji was not in line to become emperor himself. In this way, the emperor made sure that Genji could not be seen as a threat to his other relatives who wanted to be emperor. In Lady Murasaki's story, Genji grows up to be a very handsome young man. He enjoys both happy and sad times. The novel tells about his romantic adventures with a number of women—some married, some not married, and some women who were part of the royal court. Murasaki Shikibu describes these women in detail.

Lady Murasaki Shikibu wrote about the aristocracy in *The Tale of Genji*. This re-creation of a painting shows how the people in the aristocracy lived very comfortable lives.

12

The characters in *The Tale of Genji* probably are based on people Lady Murasaki knew at court. Her novel reveals the women's talents in art, music, and poetry. It includes Buddhist teachings and themes. For example, there is always a strong sense that material things do not last. This is a basic teaching of **Buddhism**. She also describes the beauty of nature—the change of seasons, the music of birds singing, and the clap of thunder. In this way, she reveals a great deal of information about Japanese culture during the Heian period.

The Tale of Genji is a long, complicated novel. It has 54 chapters and is more than 1,100 pages long. The action takes place over a 75-year period, and there are more than 400 characters to follow! Little is known about the last years of Murasaki Shikibu. Historians believe she entered religious life in a **convent**. No one knows for sure what happened to her. Some historians believe she died around 1016. Others think she died around 1026. Regardless of the details of her life and death, *The Tale of Genji* represents Murasaki Shikibu's gift to the modern world—a wonderful story that gives modern readers a view of a unique period in Japanese history.

Buddhism: a belief system that emphasizes freedom from wanting worldly possessions or power

convent: a place where a community of nuns lives

This is a color woodcut created in 1852 by artist Hiroshige Utagawa. It is called "Genji monogatari 54." It is a scene from chapter 54 of *The Tale of Genji*. Kaoru (the son of Genji's wife, the Third Princess) finds out that his lost love, Ukifune, is living at a convent nearby. He sends her younger brother to see her and give her a letter.

This is a re-creation of a painting that shows Prince Genji walking in a garden in Kyoto, while two finely dressed ladies of the court watch.

Look to the Source

You can read the first part of Lady Murasaki Shikibu's novel below. This translated excerpt tells how the emperor felt about Genji's mother. This sets the stage for the story of Genji.

enmity: the feelings of an enemy; hostility

favored: privileged or indulged; treated specially

heir apparent: a person who is believed to be entitled to receive an estate, title, or office after someone dies

molest: to annoy or bother

vie: to compete

"At the Court of an Emperor ... there was among the many gentlewomen of the Wardrobe and Chamber one, who though she was not of very high rank was **favored** far beyond all the rest. ... Thus, her position at Court ... exposed her to constant jealousy and ill will; and soon ... she fell into a decline, ... But the Emperor ... grew every day more tender ... till his conduct became the talk of all the land; ... Yet, for all this discontent, so great was the sheltering power of her master's love that none dared openly **molest** her.

Her father, who had been a Councillor, was dead. Her mother ... managed despite all difficulties to give her as good an upbringing as generally falls to the lot of young ladies whose parents are alive and at the height of fortune. ... But to return to the daughter. In due time she bore him a little Prince who ... turned out as fine and likely a man-child as well might be in all the land. The Emperor could hardly contain himself during the days of waiting. But when ... the child was presented at Court, he saw that rumor had not exaggerated its beauty. His eldest born prince was the son of Lady Kokiden, the daughter of the Minister of the Right, and this child was treated by all with the respect due to an undoubted **Heir Apparent**. But he was not so fine a child as the new prince; moreover the Emperor's great affection for the new child's mother made him feel the boy to be in a peculiar sense his own possession.

Seeing the Emperor's preference for his mistress and their son, Lady Kokiden began to fear that the new prince might become heir instead of her son. Everyone knew that the Emperor would protect his mistress from harm, but he could not protect her from the mean tricks people played to embarrass and humiliate her. Over time, this made the Emperor's mistress very ill. She ... asked the Emperor to let her go home, but he could not bear to let her go.

Finally, when the young prince was about three years old, she died. ... The Emperor thought about making the boy his heir. However, he decided against it because of the problems it would create in the Court and the land. Instead, he made the boy a member of the 'Genji' clan. That meant he had an important position in society, but could not become emperor.

Genji ('he of the Minamoto clan'), as he was now called, was constantly at the Emperor's side. He was soon quite at his ease with the common run of Ladies in Waiting and Ladies of the Wardrobe, so it was not likely he would be shy with one who was daily summoned to the Emperor's apartments. It was but natural that all these ladies should **vie** eagerly with one another for the first place in Genji's affections, and there were many whom in various ways he admired very much. But most of them behaved in too grown-up a fashion; only one, the new princess, was pretty and quite young as well. ... Kokiden had never loved this lady too well, and now her old **enmity** to Genji sprang up again; her own children were reckoned to be of quite uncommon beauty, but in this they were no match for Genji, who was so lovely a boy that people called him Hikaru Genji or Genji the Shining One."

Quick Quiz

1. True or False: Murasaki Shikibu's father only allowed her to learn etiquette.
2. What advantages in life did Genji have?
3. Why do people write diaries, poems, and novels?
4. Why do you think Murasaki Shikibu may have had to hide her knowledge?

Dante Aligheri

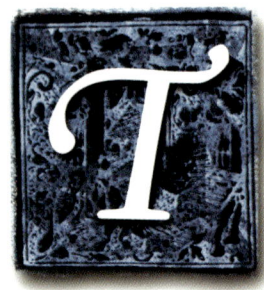

The ancient Roman Empire dominated Europe for almost 500 years. After the Western Roman Empire lost power in 476, there was no longer a central government or economic system. In the following years, Europe broke into separate kingdoms and empires. This period in European history—the time after the fall of Rome until about 1350—is called the Middle Ages. One of the greatest writers the world has ever known, the man we call Dante, lived during the late Middle Ages. Many consider his work, *The Divine Comedy*, the greatest piece of literature of all time. It is both a description of the state of a man's soul after death and a story of how human beings search for a way to be saved from their sins. Dante's work continues to have an important influence on people today.

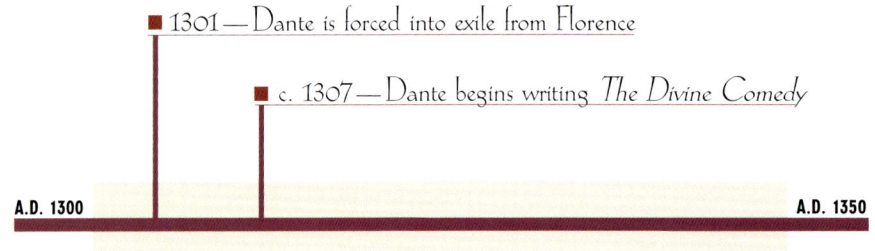

- 1301—Dante is forced into exile from Florence
- c. 1307—Dante begins writing *The Divine Comedy*

A.D. 1300 — A.D. 1350

18

Some consider Dante's *The Divine Comedy* one of the greatest works of literature. Scholars added the word "divine" to the title of Dante's story because it was about spiritual matters and also because they thought it was so well written.

Fast Facts

NAME: Dante Aligheri
BORN: 1265 in Florence, Italy
DIED: 1321 in Ravenna, Italy
FAMOUS WORKS: *The Divine Comedy; Vita Nuova; Convivio*

baptize: to dip in water or sprinkle with water; some people baptize their babies to make them a part of the Christian Church and give them a new Christian name

Learning from Life

Dante Aligheri was born in Florence, Italy, in 1265 to a prosperous family. In the early months of his life, he was known as Durante. When he was **baptized**, his family shortened his name to Dante. His father made a good living renting property in the city of Florence. His mother came from a wealthy family. Dante's parents had one other child—a girl. When Dante was seven years old, in 1272, his mother died. His father remarried and the new couple had another son and two more daughters. Dante was very close to his half brother for his entire life.

Dante began going to school when he was about seven or eight years old. He studied at a local school and learned mathematics, Latin, and logic. He may have had a private tutor as well. The schools of the time were small and damp. Most likely, his classroom was very crowded, too. Dante's education, however, was not limited to his schooling. Florence was a busy and growing city. Dante learned many things just by walking around town and talking to the people he met. We know this because in his writing, he makes many references to the different groups of people who lived in Florence during his childhood.

Exiled!

The period of time in which Dante lived was filled with political and military conflicts. Dante was greatly influenced by these conflicts.

When he grew older, he was both a soldier and a politician in defense of his native Florence. Dante was angered by and spoke out against the corruption of the **Roman Catholic Church** and the political fighting he saw in Florence. By 1301, Dante's political rivals had forced him into **exile** from Florence.

For the next 20 years, during his exile, Dante lived in several cities within Italy, many times as the guest of local noblemen. Early in his exile, he considered joining with others to raise an army and capture Florence from his enemies. Years later, the government of Florence offered him a way to return to his beloved city—he only had to confess his guilt. However, Dante would not submit to this political pressure, and he never returned to Florence. His later years were spent in the city of Ravenna. In 1321, officials of the government of Ravenna asked him to help end a disagreement with Venice over a shipping accident. Dante went to Venice, and on his way back home, he became sick with a disease called malaria and died at the age of 56.

Dante was born in Florence, Italy, a busy and growing city.

The Divine Comedy

Dante began writing *The Divine Comedy* around 1307 during his exile from Florence. The poem is set in the year 1300 and tells the story of Dante's imaginary journey as he travels through the afterlife in the *Inferno* (hell), *Purgatorio* (purgatory), and *Paradiso* (heaven). One purpose of the poem was to describe the condition of human souls after their death. Another purpose was to describe the process of religious **conversion** and **salvation**. Because the church was central in almost everyone's life during the Middle Ages, seeking religious salvation was important.

conversion: the act of changing to a new religion, faith, or belief

exile: forced removal from one's native country

Roman Catholic Church: The Christian Church split into two churches in 1054; the Christian Church in the western part of the Roman Empire became known as the "Roman Catholic Church"

salvation: saving of the soul from sin and its consequences; the state of being saved

humanity: the human race

pilgrim: a religious person who journeys to a sacred place

In the poem, Dante the **Pilgrim** represents **humanity** as he journeys through the three levels of the afterlife. In this journey, he travels through hell—a place Christians believe very sinful people go after they die. He also visits purgatory. At that time, Christians thought some people would go to a place called purgatory for a little while after they die. They would spend time there to pay for their sins. After purgatory, Christians believed people could go to heaven, or "paradise," which is the third level of the afterlife.

Virgil, a famous ancient Roman poet who lived from about 70 to 19 B.C., serves as Dante's guide on most of the journey through the afterlife. Virgil's most famous work was the epic poem *The Aeneid*. This poem was very popular with Romans because it told the story of the founding of Rome in a way that glorified the city, Emperor Augustus, and the citizens of Rome. Dante thought highly of Virgil, and *The Divine Comedy* is similar to a part of Virgil's *The Aeneid*. In *The Divine Comedy*, Virgil represents "human reason" as he guides Dante through the first two-thirds of his journey.

Dante's Journey to Meet God

Dante's poem is full of many people he knew in Florence, many people from the Christian Church, and figures from ancient mythology. Throughout the poem, Dante placed these people in different levels of hell, purgatory, or heaven. As Virgil and Dante travel through the different levels of hell and purgatory, they see the souls of sinners being given various punishments. In the last part of the poem, a woman named Beatrice meets Dante and becomes his guide through heaven. Dante knew a girl named Beatrice when he was a boy. He had loved Beatrice throughout his life. Beatrice had died at a young age. Dante wrote about her in *The Divine Comedy* and in his other works before his death in 1321. In *The Divine Comedy*, Beatrice represents God's love. Accompanied by Beatrice, Dante meets God at the end of his story.

Beatrice was Dante's guide in his imaginary journey through paradise.

Look to the Source

The Divine Comedy begins on the eve of **Good Friday** in 1300. The story covers seven days. It is written in three parts, or cantos (*Inferno*, *Purgatorio*, and *Paradiso*). Dante wrote his story in Italian and called it a "comedy" because it had a happy ending. It was unusual during this time for a work of literature to be written in Italian. Most works of literature were written in Latin, which was the common language of scholars. Below are the opening lines of the first canto (translated into English). Dante invented a rhyming pattern called "terza rima" in which the middle line of the first three lines rhymes with the first and third line of the next three lines. For example, the word *dark* rhymes with *embark* and *stark*. (The line numbers are shown to the left of the poem.)

agitation: a state of being extremely upset or disturbed

cavern: a large cave or hollow area

convey: to communicate or make known

embark: to begin

fortuitous conjunction: happy coincidence

Good Friday: the Friday before Easter

ravenous: extremely hungry

1 In the middle of our life's way
     I found myself in a wood so dark
 That I couldn't tell where the straight path lay
4 Oh how hard a thing it is to **embark**
     Upon the story of that savage wood,
 For the memory shudders me with fear so stark
7 That death itself is hardly a more bitter fruit
     Yet whatever I observed there I'll **convey**
 In order to tell what I found that was good.
10 So full of sleep was I when I left the true way
     That exactly how I entered that wild place
 It's impossible for me to say;
13 But when I'd cleared that dark space
     Which had turned my heart into a **cavern**
 Of fear, I found myself at the base
16 Of a hill upon whose shoulders I could discern
     The rays of that brilliant planet
 Which guides men straight through every turn.
19 With what relief a sense of quiet
     Was welcomed by a heart tossed all night
 So piteously, surely I can never forget.

Quick Quiz

1. On what day does *The Divine Comedy* begin?
2. What is the name of Dante's first guide during his journey in *The Divine Comedy*?
3. How does this excerpt help you learn about the culture and history of Europe during the Middle Ages?
4. Why is a common language(s) for scholars important? Why is Latin no longer the language of scholars? Is there a language of scholars today? Explain your answer.

This statue of Dante stands outside the Basilica of Santa Croce in Florence, Italy.

22 And like a man who, reaching shore, turns his sight
    Still shivering upon the raging sea
From whose clutch he's just made frantic flight.
25 So my spirit, driven even now to flee,
    Looked back at that pass which had never
Let a single living soul go free.
28 When I had let my tired body recover,
    And was once more on the lonely slope, I found
That for balance my firm foot was forever
31 Lower than the other on the ground.
    But then suddenly!—at the start of a steep ascent
There appeared a spotted leopard, jumping all around.
34 With great nimbleness and plain intent
    To block my path. The hour was early morning,
And rising with the sun were those very stars present
37 When Divine Love first breathed life into each fair thing;
    Such a **fortuitous conjunction**
Of time and sweet season sent my hopes soaring,
40 Until I was thrown into **agitation**
    By the sudden, stunning sight
Of a fierce, **ravenous** lion.

Leo Africanus

Africa is the second largest continent on earth. It is 5,000 miles from north to south and 4,600 miles from east to west. In ancient times, it was possible to get to North Africa by land or sea from Europe and Asia. As a result, the people of North Africa were involved in trade, wars, and cultural exchanges with people from Europe and Asia. The people of eastern and southern Africa also had contact with people from the eastern Mediterranean and from parts of Asia. The people of West Africa, however, were more isolated from Europe and Asia because it was difficult for travelers to get to West Africa. One of the earliest, most complete accounts Europeans had of West Africa came from a 16th-century traveler and historian from Spain known by the name of Leo Africanus.

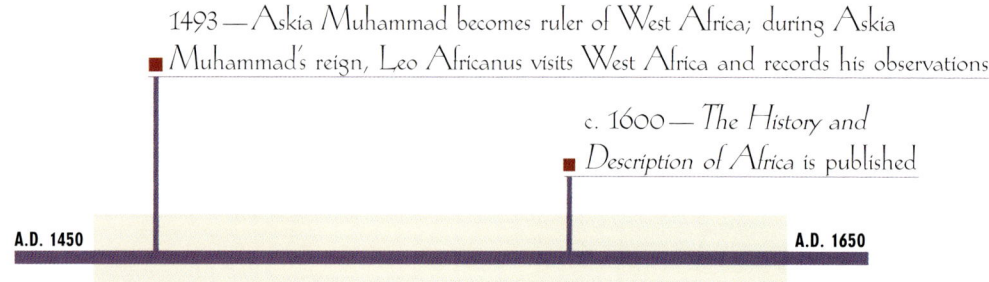

1493 — Askia Muhammad becomes ruler of West Africa; during Askia Muhammad's reign, Leo Africanus visits West Africa and records his observations

c. 1600 — *The History and Description of Africa* is published

A.D. 1450 — A.D. 1650

Leo Africanus's *The History and Description of Africa* helped inform Europeans about West Africa.

27

Fast Facts

NAME: Hassan Ibn Muhammad, but he is known popularly as Leo Africanus
BORN: late 1400s in Spain
DIED: mid-1500s in Tunis, North Africa
FAMOUS WORK: *The History and Description of Africa*

The Sahara Desert— An Obstacle for Travelers

West African people had close contact with one another. Before the 700s, however, they did not have very much contact with people in other parts of the world. At that time, no one knew how to sail against the wind. This meant that ships could not land on the west coast of Africa. Also, the Sahara—a huge, dry, and sandy desert—made land travel to West Africa difficult and dangerous.

About 5,000-7,000 years ago, the area we call the Sahara desert was a tropical environment. Then the climate changed. By about 2500 B.C., the Sahara had become a huge, dry, and sandy desert.

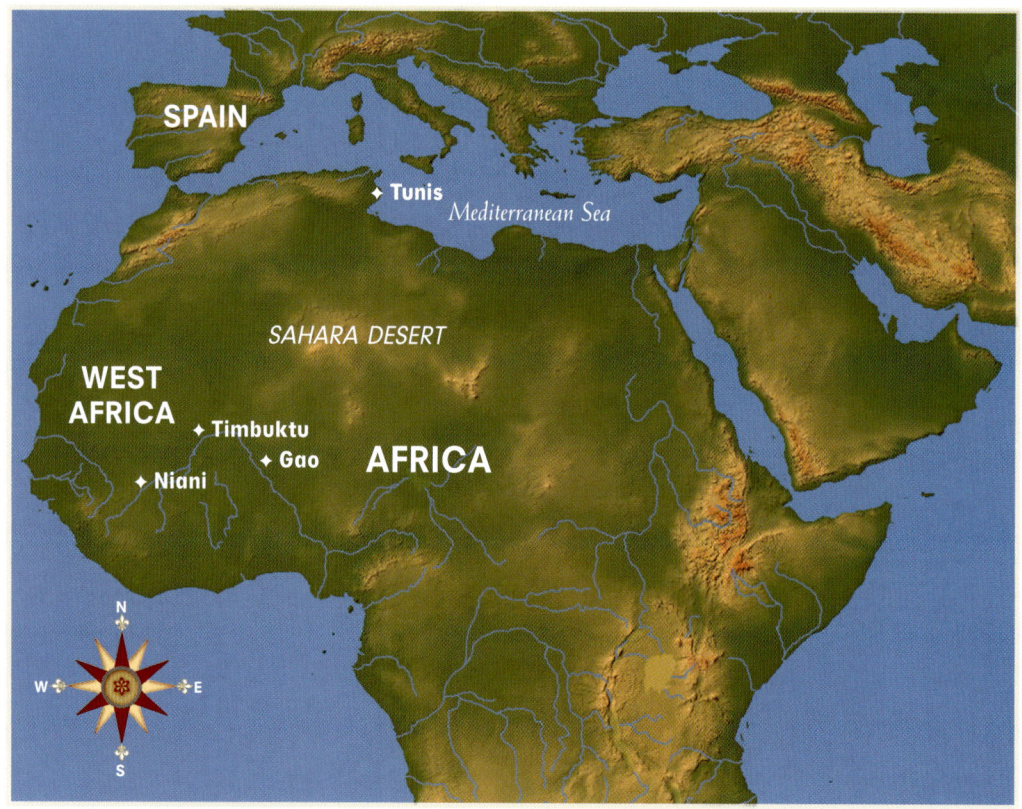

28

As West Africans began to trade their surplus goods, including gold, with other groups, people in other parts of the world began to see the riches of West Africa.

After the **Muslims** conquered northwest Africa in the 600s, traders and merchants traveled across the Sahara desert into West Africa. By the late 700s, camel caravans were making regular trips across the Sahara to West Africa. Various West African kingdoms grew more powerful and then declined. By the mid-1400s, Songhai was the dominant West African power. In 1493, Askia Muhammad became ruler of this kingdom. During Askia Muhammad's reign, Muslim writer Leo Africanus visited West Africa and recorded his ideas about what he saw.

Travels in Africa

We do not have much information about the early life of Leo Africanus. We know he was born in Spain in the late 1400s and that his parents named him Hassan Ibn Muhammad. He must have received a good education and had an interest in traveling to faraway places. Like other Muslim travelers and traders, he served as an **ambassador** for some West African leaders. On one of his visits, he traveled to the West African city of Timbuktu. He described the city as having "a splendid and well-organized royal court, many craftsmen's shops, and markets where European cloth is sold." He said Timbuktu was a bustling city filled with scholars, a busy market, and a fine stone palace for the king. Timbuktu, he said, was "bountifully maintained at the king's cost." He described Niani, the capital of the kingdom of Mali, as a town that had about 6,000 houses, several **mosques**, and schools to teach **Islam**. He said the people of Mali were superior to "all other **Negroes** in wit, civility, and industry."

ambassador: a person of a high status who represents one government to another

Islam: a religion based on the teachings of the prophet Muhammad

mosque: a Muslim place of worship

Muslim: a follower of Islam

Negro: a person with dark skin from Africa; now considered to be an insulting term

Look to the Source

ducat: any of various gold coins formerly used in European countries

wares: goods; articles for sale

Leo Africanus's Impressions of the City of Gao:

"Gao is a very large city ... without surrounding walls. ... Most of its houses are ugly; however, a few, in which live the king and his court, have a very fine aspect. Its inhabitants are rich merchants who travel constantly about the region with their **wares**. A great many Blacks come to the city bringing quantities of gold with which to purchase goods imported from the Berber country [in North Africa] and from Europe, but they never find enough goods on which to spend all their gold and always take half or two-thirds of it home.

The city is well-policed in comparison to Timbuktu. Bread and meat exist in great abundance, but one can find neither wine nor fruit. In truth, melons, cucumbers, and excellent pumpkins are abundant and they have enormous quantities of rice.

The people of West Africa used gold for jewelry, masks, and decorations. People even wore cloth made with golden thread.

Freshwater wells are numerous. There is a place where they sell countless ... slaves on market days. A fifteen-year-old girl is worth about six **ducats** and a young man nearly as much; little children and aged slaves are worth about half that sum.

The king has a special palace set aside for women, concubines, and slaves, ... He has ... a necessary guard of horsemen and of foot-soldiers armed with bows. Between the public gate and the private door to his palace is a great courtyard surrounded by a wall. A gallery on each side is used for holding audiences. Even though the king handles all his affairs himself, he is aided by many ... secretaries, advisors, captains, and stewards."

When pirates captured him, Leo Africanus was carrying a draft of a book called *The History and Description of Africa and of the Notable Things Therein Contained*. This work was translated into English and published in London around 1600.

Pirates and a Pope

Hassan Ibn Muhammad had many exciting adventures while he was traveling in Africa. His journey home to Spain was similarly eventful. Christian pirates in the Mediterranean Sea attacked the ship on which he was sailing. The pirates did not want to harm him because they thought he had valuable knowledge that might be worth a **ransom**. They took him to Rome to see Pope Leo X, the leader of the Roman Catholic Church.

Leo Africanus and *The History and Description of Africa*

Pope Leo was excited to hear the stories Hassan Ibn Muhammad told about his experiences in Africa. The pope gave him a new name—Leo Africanus—and enough money so that he could spend his time writing about his African experiences. His book, *The History and Description of Africa*, provides a written account of these experiences. Leo Africanus made it clear that the wealthy West African kingdoms highly prized European goods. They were eager to trade their gold and ivory for European cloth, books, and other manufactured goods. Historians believe Leo Africanus died in the mid-1500s in Tunis, North Africa. The stories he told encouraged European traders and travelers to take notice of this area of the world. Leo Africanus's words had far-reaching consequences for both Europe and West Africa.

This is a modern-day portrait of Pope Leo X, based on a famous painting by the artist Raphael (1483-1520). Pope Leo X was excited to hear the stories Hassan Ibn Muhammad told about his experiences in Africa.

ransom: a payment made to release a hostage

Quick Quiz

1. What was Leo Africanus's name and occupation when he lived in Spain?
2. According to Leo Africanus, who are Gao's inhabitants and what do they do?
3. Why do you think the pope gave Hassan Ibn Muhammad the name "Leo Africanus"?
4. What was the economic problem in Gao's market—too much supply or too much demand? Explain your answer.

Bartolomé de las Casas

During the European age of exploration, Spain's explorers came into contact with highly developed civilizations in the Americas and claimed the new lands on behalf of Spain. These new lands became Spanish colonies. By the early 1500s, Spain ruled a large part of North and South America, and had power and authority over the people who lived there. Much of the information we have about the people who lived in the Americas during this time comes from accounts written by Spanish conquerors, soldiers, and Christian missionaries. One of these missionaries was a man named Bartolomé de las Casas. During his lifetime, King Charles V of Spain awarded him the title *Defensor de los Indios* or "Defender of the Indians." It was a title Bartolomé de las Casas had surely earned as the man who led the first major fight for the rights of the powerless people in the Americas.

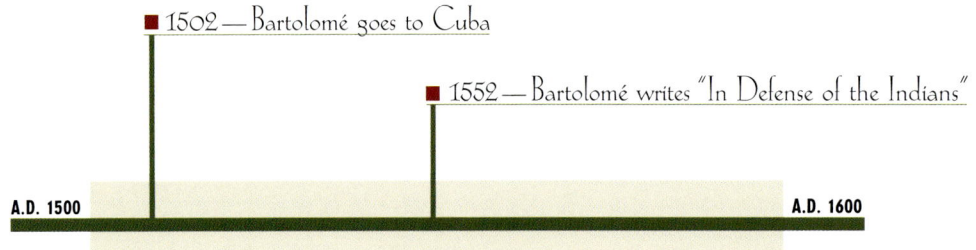

One historian commented that las Casas risked "his reputation and even life, but he never tired."

Fast Facts

NAME: Bartolomé de las Casas
BORN: 1474 in Seville, Spain
DIED: 1566 in Madrid, Spain
FAMOUS WORKS: "In Defense of the Indians"; *History of the Indies*

discrimination: treatment based on class, race, or other category

New World: the term once used to describe North and South America

The Life of Bartolomé de las Casas

Bartolomé de las Casas was only 18 years old when Christopher Columbus sailed across the Atlantic Ocean to the continent that Europeans did not know existed. Las Casas admired the courage, determination, and intelligence of Columbus and other early explorers. Today, it might be argued that Bartolomé de las Casas possessed these very same qualities. However, Bartolomé de las Casas's courage, determination, and intelligence were not focused on exploration, adventure, and conquest. Instead, he wrote powerful books and essays, and spoke out against the **discrimination**, cruelty, and intolerance the Spanish conquerors directed toward the Indians of the **New World**. Bartolomé de las Casas led a brave, unpopular, and often lonely fight to protect the people Spain had conquered in the Americas.

Bartolomé de las Casas left Spain for Cuba in 1502.

36

A Priest in the Americas

Not much is known about the early life of Bartolomé de las Casas. We know he was born in Seville, Spain, in 1474 and sailed to the New World in 1502. At first, he went to Hispaniola where he had an "encomienda"—a large estate and the service of all the Indians living there. Later, he helped conquer Cuba and was awarded another large encomienda there. By about 1513, Bartolomé de las Casas had become a priest. Historians think he was the first person in the Americas to become a Roman Catholic priest. Around 1514, he decided to set free the Indians who were **serfs** on his estates. He also began to preach against the encomienda system.

serf: a peasant worker who must work for a landowner and who may not quit or leave the land without permission

A Champion of the Indians

During this time, Spain was very eager to get as many riches from the Americas as possible. Some Spaniards were concerned about converting the Indians of the Americas to Christianity, but most were more interested in becoming wealthy and powerful. Many saw only the positive consequences of the encomienda system, which helped them become rich. However, Bartolomé de las Casas believed very strongly that the Indians were not property. He believed they should be treated as human beings. He did not think the Indians were inferior to Europeans. He thought they had rights and that their cultural traditions should be respected. Many wealthy and powerful Spaniards disagreed with las Casas. They thought the Indians were inferior to the Spaniards, in the same way they believed children were inferior to adults and women were inferior to men. Some Spaniards thought las Casas was a traitor because he was such a strong defender of the Indians.

Speaking on Behalf of the Indians

Francisco Pizarro and his men conquered and destroyed the Inca empire in South America.

Bartolomé de las Casas argued in the Americas and in Spain on behalf of the Indians. He traveled to Spain on many occasions and tried to convince Spanish leaders that the Indians should be treated as human beings. Las Casas encouraged the passage of laws in Spain to protect the rights of Indians in the Americas. In 1522, he joined the Dominican order of missionaries. By 1545, he was appointed bishop in present-day Guatemala. He wanted to convert the people of the Americas to Christianity, but believed Christianity should be introduced peacefully.

Bartolomé de las Casas wrote to the king of Spain about the terrible injustices that were being done in the Americas by conquistadors such as Hernando Cortés and Francisco Pizarro and their soldiers. For example, this is how he described the behavior of Pedro de Alvarado, an officer in Cortés's army: "He advanced killing, ravaging, burning, robbing, and destroying all the country wherever he came." In 1527, Bartolomé de las Casas began writing *History of the Indies*. He returned to Spain for the last time in 1547 and died in Madrid in 1566. *History of the Indies* began circulating almost right away. Soon it was translated into English and people throughout Europe began to read it. It continues to be influential today. In 1942, Samuel Eliot Morison, a distinguished American historian, called it "the one book on the discovery of America that I should wish to preserve if all others were destroyed."

Quick Quiz

1. Why did las Casas write a letter to the king of Spain?
2. True or False: Las Casas probably had great respect and admiration for European explorers such as Cortés and Pizarro. Explain your answer.
3. How does the excerpt on the next page help you learn about the culture and history of Europe during the age of exploration? How does it help you learn about the culture and history of the Americas at that time?
4. Why do you think las Casas was concerned about Spain's treatment of the Indians?

Look to the Source

Below, you can read a translated excerpt from Bartolomé de las Casas's "In Defense of the Indians." Bartolomé de las Casas wrote these words in 1552.

destitute: lacking
impart: to teach
plunder: to rob or steal goods, especially in time of war
slaughter: to kill
temperate: moderate

"... What man of sound mind will approve a war against men [referring to the natives of the New World that the Spanish called 'Indians'] who are harmless, ignorant, gentle, **temperate**, unarmed, and **destitute** of every human defense? For the results of such a war are very surely the loss of the souls of that people who perish without knowing God ... and, for the survivors, hatred and loathing of the Christian religion. ... What will these people think of Christ, the true God of the Christians, when they see Christians venting their rage against them with so many massacres, so much bloodshed without any just cause? ...

... How will they become our friends (which is necessary if they are to accept our religion), when children see themselves deprived of parents, wives of husbands, and fathers of children and friends? When they see those they love wounded, imprisoned, **plundered**, and reduced from an immense number to a few? When they see their rulers stripped of their authority, ... Who is there who would want the gospel preached to himself in such a fashion?

... 'So always treat others as you would like them to treat you.' This is something that every man knows, grasps, and understands by the natural light that has been **imparted** to our minds. ... Consider that war and the massacre of this timid race [the Indians of the Americas] has lasted, not for one day or a hundred days, but for ten or twenty years, to the incredible harm of the natives; that as they wander about, hidden and scattered through the woods and forests, unarmed, naked, deprived of every human help, they are **slaughtered** by the Spaniards. ... In the absolutely inhuman things they [the Spaniards] have done to those nations [the native people of the Americas] they have surpassed all other barbarians."

Bartolomé de las Casas tried to convince Spanish leaders that the Indians should be treated as human beings. This statue shows las Casas and an Indian. It stands in Madrid, Spain.

Miguel Cervantes

Miguel Cervantes did not come from a wealthy family or receive a fine education. He was mostly self-taught as a boy, and when he was older he lost the use of one hand. Throughout his life, Miguel Cervantes was often poor, sometimes imprisoned, and generally a failure in most of the things he tried to do. It seems unlikely, then, that he would become one of Spain's greatest literary heroes. But that is exactly what he did. He achieved great fame late in life because of his book, *Don Quixote de la Mancha*.

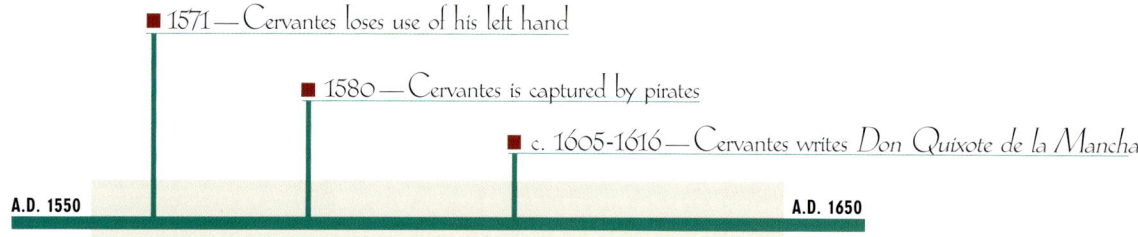

Cervantes is considered one of Spain's greatest literary heroes.

Fast Facts

NAME: Miguel Cervantes
BORN: 1547 in Alcálá de Henares, Spain
DIED: 1616
FAMOUS WORK: *Don Quixote de la Mancha*

The Renaissance

Europe was an exciting place to live during the period from about 1350 to the 1600s. Major cultural, religious, and scientific changes were taking place in European society. Historians call this period of European history the Renaissance. During this period, people began to look more critically at Christian Church teachings and at ideas about politics, religion, and education. They were interested in learning about the ideas of the ancient Romans and Greeks. However, they also developed their own new ideas, which slowly began to change European society. Some people thought it was as if society was being reborn. This "rebirth," or Renaissance, started in Italy but by the mid-1500s, the ideas of the Italian Renaissance had become popular throughout Europe. People outside Italy adapted these Renaissance ideas according to their own traditions. They were interested in bringing together ancient ideas of human reason with religious themes. They wanted to create art and literature that was realistic and full of human passion.

Miguel Cervantes was born in Alcála de Henares, a small town outside Madrid, Spain.

Early Life

Miguel Cervantes was born in Alcála de Henares, a small town outside Madrid, Spain, in 1547. No one knows his exact birth date. Some historians think it was September 29, St. Michael's Day. His parents were not wealthy and they already had two daughters. However, they must have been pleased to welcome a son into their family and to baptize him Miguel on October 16, 1547. He lived with his family in Alcála de Henares until they moved to Córdoba when he was about six years old.

Miguel probably made friends with other boys his age, played on the banks of the Guadalquivir River, watched puppet shows in the square, walked across the ancient Roman bridge, and attended school for a while. The family moved again, first to a small town outside Córdoba in 1557, and then to the city of Seville around 1564. In 1566, when Miguel was about 19 years old, they headed for Madrid so Miguel's father could go to court to collect an inheritance he thought he was owed. Miguel made friends in Madrid with some poets and other writers. He also began to write poetry himself, but his poems were never considered very good. It appears that he got into trouble with the law in 1569 and had to leave Madrid very quickly.

Florence, Italy (shown below), was considered the birthplace of the Renaissance. During the same time the Renaissance was happening in Italy, Spain was having a Renaissance of its own.

chivalry: how a knight must act—with respect for the church, pity for the poor, bravery, and courtesy

No one knows for certain, but it seems likely that Cervantes fled to Italy. He found work in an Italian noble's home, but as a young man in his early 20s, he was eager for adventure. He may have thought that joining the military was a way to support himself. In his book, *Don Quixote de la Mancha*, Cervantes wrote, "My poverty leads me to war, but, you know, if I had any money I never would go."

The Life of a Soldier

Miguel Cervantes became a soldier and fought with the Spanish army. He sailed from Italy to Lepanto in Greece. The conditions aboard the ship were terrible. But the real misery came during the battle of Lepanto in 1571. It is said, "In a strip of sea less than five miles across and a few hundred yards deep, more than sixty thousand fighting men hacked and flailed with swords, pikes, daggers, maces, javelins." Cervantes was wounded three times in the battle of Lepanto, and he lost the use of his left hand. However, that did not stop him. He fought in another battle—this time against Muslims in North Africa. In 1580, as he was returning to Spain, pirates captured him and demanded a ransom for his release. After his ransom was paid, Cervantes returned to Madrid. He had various government jobs, but was not very successful at any of them. His personal life was not very happy or successful either.

Cervantes's Personal Renaissance

In his late 50s and throughout his 60s, Cervantes seemed to find his own personal "rebirth," or Renaissance. He wrote *Don Quixote de la Mancha*, which became hugely successful throughout Europe. His story was a parody—a comic imitation—of the romantic tales of **chivalry** that had been very popular. In Cervantes's story, the chivalrous knight was out of his mind, but he was very sincere. The effect is a tragic but funny story. Many of the incidents that occur in the book are based on Cervantes's own life experiences. Before his death in 1616, Miguel Cervantes wrote other works of literature, but his fame is tied to his masterpiece, *Don Quixote de la Mancha*.

Don Quixote de la Mancha is a story of a knight. This scene shows Don Quixote in one of his many adventures. He is attached to a line held by another man and is preparing to enter a cave.

Look to the Source

Below, you can read a translated excerpt from *Don Quixote de la Mancha*. In this passage, Cervantes is giving the reader some background information to explain why the main character, the gentleman who eventually named himself Don Quixote, went out of his mind and began to roam the countryside like the knights of the Middle Ages.

immersed: deeply involved

infatuation: an intense, temporary love

pore: to read or study carefully

robust constitution: healthy body

tillable: able to be plowed and used for agriculture

torment: pain

"This gentleman of ours was close to fifty, of a **robust constitution** but with little flesh on his bones and a face that was lean. … the aforesaid gentleman, on those occasions when he was at leisure, which was most of the year round, was in the habit of reading books of chivalry with such pleasure and devotion as to lead him almost wholly to forget … even the administration of his estate. So great was his curiosity and **infatuation** in this regard that he even sold many acres of **tillable** land in order to be able to buy and read the books that he loved, and he would carry home with him as many of them as he could obtain …

In short, our gentleman became so **immersed** in his reading that he spent whole nights from sundown to sunup and his days from dawn to dusk in **poring** over his books, until, finally, from so little sleeping and so much reading, his brain dried up and he went completely out of his mind. He had filled his imagination with everything that he had read, with enchantments, knightly encounters, battles, challenges, wounds, with tales of love and its **torments**, and all sorts of impossible things, and as a result had come to believe that all these fictitious happenings were true; they were more real to him than anything else in the world."

Here, Don Quixote is sitting under a tree with shepherds. One of the shepherds is playing an instrument.

Quick Quiz

1. What is a parody?
2. What caused Don Quixote to go out of his mind?
3. How does this excerpt help you learn about the culture and history of Europe during the Renaissance?
4. Why do you think the main character in the story became so involved in books of chivalry and created his own fantasy world? Do people today create their own fantasy worlds? Explain your answer.

William Shakespeare

"O Romeo, Romeo! Wherefore art thou Romeo?" Chances are, you have heard this line from William Shakespeare's play *Romeo and Juliet*. Some of the many poems he wrote also may be familiar to you.

We do not know much about Shakespeare's early life. However, we know that later in his life he became a playwright and wrote some plays that were funny and some that were serious. Shakespeare wrote and performed plays for royalty, including Queen Elizabeth I of England. These plays included serious tragedies such as *Romeo and Juliet*, *Hamlet*, and *Othello*, and light-hearted comedies such as *Much Ado about Nothing* and *As You Like It*. Shakespeare wrote 38 plays in all! Throughout the Western world, William Shakespeare is considered by many to be the greatest playwright who ever lived.

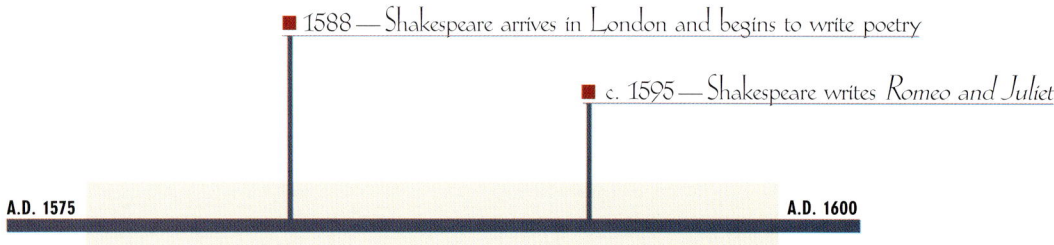

- 1588 — Shakespeare arrives in London and begins to write poetry
- c. 1595 — Shakespeare writes *Romeo and Juliet*

A.D. 1575 — A.D. 1600

Shakespeare is often considered the greatest playwright who ever lived.

Fast Facts

NAME: William Shakespeare
BORN: c. 1564 in Stratford-upon-Avon, England
DIED: 1616
FAMOUS WORKS: Many sonnets and 38 plays, including *Romeo and Juliet*, *As You Like It*, and *Much Ado about Nothing*

Early Life

William Shakespeare was born in a little town in England called Stratford-upon-Avon, about 65 miles northwest of London. People say Shakespeare was born on April 23, 1564. We know he was baptized on April 24, 1564 because there is a church record of this event. William was the third of eight children and the oldest son in the Shakespeare family. His father, John Shakespeare, was a glovemaker and merchant in the town. His mother, Mary, was from a wealthy, land-owning family. We think young William went to school in town where he learned to read and write.

William Shakespeare lived in England during the Renaissance.

Merchant? Apprentice? Hunter?

As he got older, William probably began to learn something about business. During that time, boys often trained to do the same kind of work as their fathers. William was probably expected to become a businessman. However, we don't know this for sure. Some people believe he became a teacher. Another story says he became an **apprentice** to a butcher. The plays he wrote later in his life include a great deal of information about hunting, so historians think he may have had free time when he was growing up and spent time in the forests and fields going on hunts. Church records tell us that William Shakespeare married Anne Hathaway, the daughter of a farmer, in 1582. They soon began their family. They had a daughter in 1583 and twins (a boy and a girl) in 1585.

apprentice: a beginning learner of a job

Writing Sonnets

Shakespeare left Stratford-upon-Avon without his family and arrived in London in 1588. He began to write poetry that people greatly admired. He wrote a kind of poem called a sonnet. *Sonnet* comes from the Italian word *sonetto*, which means "little song." A sonnet is a type of poem that has a set form. It always has 14 lines, and the lines rhyme according to a particular pattern. In poetry, a rhyme scheme is shown by assigning a letter to each rhyme sound. The rhyme scheme for an English sonnet is abab, cdcd, efef, and gg. This means that the first and third lines rhyme, the second and fourth lines rhyme, the fifth and seventh lines rhyme, and so forth, until the end when the last two lines rhyme. In the first three parts—or stanzas—of the sonnet (abab, cdcd, efef), the poet often raises a question. The last two lines—called a couplet—present an answer or solution to the question. William Shakespeare was a master of the English sonnet. In fact, English sonnets are often referred to as Shakespearean sonnets.

Look to the Source

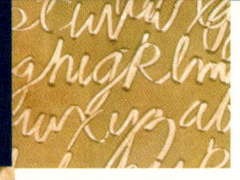

Below, you can read one of Shakespeare's most famous sonnets.

SONNET 18

LINES	RHYMING WORD	RHYMING PATTERN
Shall I compare thee to a summer's day?	day	a
Thou art more lovely and more temperate:	temperate	b
Rough winds do shake the darling buds of May,	May	a
And summer's lease hath all too short a date:	date	b
Sometime too hot the eye of heaven shines,	shines	c
And often is his gold complexion dimm'd;	dimm'd	d
And every fair from fair sometime declines,	declines	c
By chance, or nature's changing course untrimm'd;	untrimm'd	d
But thy eternal summer shall not fade,	fade	e
Nor lose possession of that fair thou ow'st;	ow'st	f
Nor shall Death brag thou wander'st in his shade,	shade	e
When in eternal lines to time thou grow'st:	grow'st	f
So long as men can breathe, or eyes can see,	see	g
So long lives this, and this gives life to thee.	thee	g

Performing for London Audiences

While in London, Shakespeare also joined a group of actors called the King's Men. This acting group often performed plays in front of the English royalty, including Queen Elizabeth I. However, Shakespeare's greatest talent was writing plays. Some of his plays are "histories." These are plays he wrote about real people in history. For example, he wrote a play about Julius Caesar, a ruler of ancient Rome. He also wrote about rulers in English history.

Tragedies

Many of Shakespeare's plays are tragedies. They tell stories about the struggle between good and evil. Tragedies usually end with the death or downfall of the main character. These plays are often very sad, but they can help us understand how not to make the same mistakes the characters made. One of Shakespeare's most famous tragedies is *Romeo and Juliet*. In this play, two young people fall in love. But their families are bitter enemies. Romeo and Juliet are caught in the middle of this family fight. In the end, both Romeo and Juliet die. We are left with the idea that hatred only causes sorrow.

" ... He was not of an age, but for all time! ... "
—Ben Jonson in a poem on *William Shakespeare*, 1623

Shakespeare joined an acting group that performed plays in front of the English royalty. This drawing shows him performing before Queen Elizabeth I and her court.

This picture shows Juliet on the balcony of her house. This is one of the most famous scenes in *Romeo and Juliet*.

Look to the Source

Below, you can read an excerpt from a scene in Shakespeare's *Romeo and Juliet*. Juliet is on the **balcony** of her house. At first, Juliet doesn't realize that Romeo is on the ground below the balcony. She is in love with him, but thinks that their love is impossible.

balcony: a platform that sticks out of the wall of a building and is surrounded by a railing

What the Characters Say:	What the Characters Mean:
JULIET: O Romeo, Romeo! Wherefore art thou Romeo? / Deny thy father and refuse thy name; / Or, if thou wilt not, be but sworn my love, / And I'll no longer be a Capulet.	Juliet calls out for Romeo. She wants him to give up his family name (Montague). If he won't do this, she says she will give up her name (Capulet).
ROMEO: (aside) Shall I hear more, or shall I speak at this?	Romeo asks himself, "Should I let Juliet know I can hear what she is saying?"
JULIET: 'Tis but thy name that is my enemy; / Thou art thyself, though not a Montague. / What's Montague? It is nor hand, nor foot, / Nor arm, nor face, nor any other part / Belonging to a man. O, be some other name! / What's in a name? That which we call a rose / By any other name would smell as sweet; ...	Juliet says that Romeo isn't her enemy. It is his name that is keeping them apart. She says she wishes he were from a different family and that he had a different last name. To make her point she asks, "Would a rose smell any differently if we called the rose by a different name?"

This is a photograph of a modern-day performance of Shakespeare's comedy, *As You Like It*. Some of the educated people of his day did not think Shakespeare's plays were proper entertainment. But his plays were very popular with most people.

58

Comedies

Not all of Shakespeare's plays are serious histories and tragedies. He also wrote many plays that are comedies. For example, *As You Like It* and *Much Ado about Nothing* are two of his comedies. A comedy is a funny play. The characters in comedies usually act **foolishly**, but the plays always have a happy ending. Most of Shakespeare's comedies end with people getting married. Like tragedies, comedies can teach us lessons about life. They can help us avoid the foolish behavior we saw in the play!

foolish: silly; lacking good judgment or common sense

Back in Stratford-upon-Avon

Around 1608, when Shakespeare was in his mid-40s, he began to spend more time at his home in Stratford-upon-Avon. He was an important person in the town. He built a beautiful home for his family and lived there until his death on April 23, 1616. He was buried at the Stratford church. Today, people still enjoy going to see Shakespeare's plays and other works based on his plays.

Quick Quiz

1. Shakespeare wrote, "That which we call a rose by any other name would smell as sweet." What does this mean? Give an example.
2. Shakespeare wrote three types of plays. What were they?
3. Do you think plays can teach us lessons about life? Explain your answer.
4. What do you think is William Shakespeare's greatest achievement? Give reasons for your answer.

Voltaire

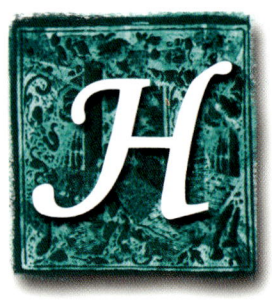

Historians refer to the period of European history that spanned the 1700s as the Enlightenment. During this time, great thinkers discussed new ideas about how people could create better societies using reason. Enlightenment ideas helped shape new forms of government, including the government of the United States of America. Enlightenment ideas also influenced agricultural and industrial revolutions in Europe and other places. During the Enlightenment, groups of people began to meet and exchange ideas. These Enlightenment thinkers were called "philosophes." The man we know as Voltaire was one of the most famous philosophes. He has been called "the wittiest writer in an age of great wits" and the man "who knew everybody who was anybody; his friends and acquaintances, who ranged from peasants to popes, have never been counted, but over 1800 of them were also his correspondents."

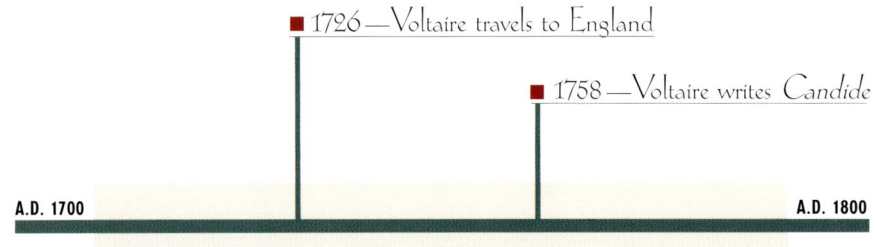

- 1726—Voltaire travels to England
- 1758—Voltaire writes *Candide*

A.D. 1700 — A.D. 1800

Voltaire was one of the most famous Enlightenment thinkers in Europe.

Fast Facts

NAME: Born François-Marie Arouet, but known popularly as Voltaire
BORN: 1694 in Paris, France
DIED: 1778
FAMOUS WORKS: *Candide* and many other works

Early Life

The man we know of as Voltaire was born François-Marie Arouet to a middle-class French family in 1694. His family was relatively wealthy, but it was not part of the French aristocracy. François-Marie was the youngest of three children. Growing up, he received an excellent education and was a brilliant student. He learned a little Latin and Greek, as well as French language, literature, and history.

Voltaire is known as one of the greatest Enlightenment thinkers. He was born in France and traveled throughout Europe.

Voltaire read the works of ancient Romans such as Cicero, Virgil, Horace, and Ovid. It was during these years that he also developed a love for the stage. His formal education ended in 1711. Later, he wrote of one of his **Jesuit** teachers, "Nothing will blot out in my heart the memory of father Porée, who is equally dear to all who studied under him. No man ever made study and virtue more agreeable. The hours of his lessons were to us delightful hours … ." At first, it seemed as if Voltaire would become a lawyer. Instead, he began writing plays and poetry.

Traveling throughout Europe

Voltaire traveled in France and then went to the Netherlands before returning to Paris. His life was not always easy. In fact, when he wrote a **satirical** essay criticizing the Roman Catholic Church and the French government, he was put in jail for almost a year. When he was released, he was forced to leave Paris. After a while, he was allowed to return and was present when his father was buried there in 1722. He continued to write and travel throughout Europe, and was gaining many admirers for his work. However, when he got into a disagreement with a French noble, his friends did not support him and he was put in prison. This experience affected him for the rest of his life. He thought the actions against him were terribly unfair and unjust.

In 1726, Voltaire was released and traveled to England where he saw the rights enjoyed by English citizens. He spoke favorably of their freedom of religion: "If one religion only were allowed in England, the government would very possibly become **arbitrary**; if there were but two, the people wou'd cut one another's throats; but as there are such a multitude, they all live happy and in peace." Eventually, Voltaire returned to France with new ideas and a growing reputation as an enlightened thinker.

arbitrary: based on or subject to individual judgment

Jesuit: a member of the Society of Jesus

satirical: witty and mocking

Emile's relationship with Voltaire caused a great deal of gossip in the French royal court and often overshadowed her work as a writer.

"Judge me for my own merits, or lack of them, but do not look upon me as a mere appendage [part] to this great general or that great scholar ... I am in my own right a whole person ... ."
—*Madame du Châtelet, in a letter to Frederick the Great of Prussia*

In Love

The woman we call Madame du Châtelet was born Gabrielle Emile Le Tonnelier de Breteuil in 1706. Her family was part of the elite French aristocracy. Known to her friends as Emile, her family expected that she would marry a French nobleman and live a traditional life. In fact, her life was anything but traditional. Her family moved to Paris and realized that Emile was a bright young girl. By the age of 12, she was being tutored in English, Latin, and Italian. Emile was very good at mathematics and science. She listened to the many intellectuals and scholars who came to visit her father.

In 1725, at the age of 19, Emile married a military officer from a prominent family. He was often away from home for long periods on military assignments. Emile, alone in Paris, began to spend time in Parisian cafés discussing ideas with the intellectuals of her time, including Voltaire. Voltaire already was a famous writer by the time he and Emile met. Although she remained married to her husband, Emile had a long, loving relationship with Voltaire.

For many years, Emile and Voltaire lived and worked in the French countryside. It was during this period of almost 16 years that Voltaire wrote many of his most important works. Under Voltaire's influence, Emile became a serious student of science and philosophy. Her greatest accomplishments came from her work in translating many of the most important writings of the Enlightenment from English into French. Emile also influenced Voltaire to take up the study of physics begun by Isaac Newton. Emile's relationship with Voltaire was not a secret, but it caused a great deal of gossip in the French royal court. Toward the end of her life, Emile stopped living with Voltaire, but they continued to be close friends.

Look to the Source

baron: a nobleman

Voltaire wrote about many different topics, including religion, science, and politics. However, his most famous work is *Candide*. Voltaire wrote this book in 1758 when he was 64 years old. He was living in Geneva, Switzerland, at the time. He said he felt safe there from attacks by the Roman Catholic Church and the French government. *Candide* tells a satirical story of an inexperienced young man who learns about intolerance and cruelty in the world. Candide's mother and father were not married. Candide promised to marry the young and beautiful Cunégonde, the sister of a powerful **baron**. However, the baron refused because Candide was not of noble birth. Later in life, Candide finds Cunégonde again. She is no longer young and beautiful. Still, Candide agrees to keep his promise to marry her. The following translated excerpt from *Candide* tells what happened next.

> "In the neighborhood there was a small farm which the old woman suggested that Candide should take, while waiting for the party's fortunes to improve. Cunégonde did not know she had grown so ugly, since no one had told her; but as she now reminded Candide of his promises with the utmost firmness, the good man did not dare to refuse her. He then informed the Baron that he was going to marry his sister.

'I shall never allow her to disgrace herself so meanly,' said the Baron, 'and I shall not permit such **insolence** from you. With that disgrace at least I shall never be reproached. My sister's children could never enter the highest ranks of German society. No, my sister shall marry none but a baron of the **Holy Roman Empire**.'

Holy Roman Empire: an empire, consisting largely of Germanic states in central and western Europe, established in 962 and ending in 1806

insolence: arrogance; insulting manner or speech

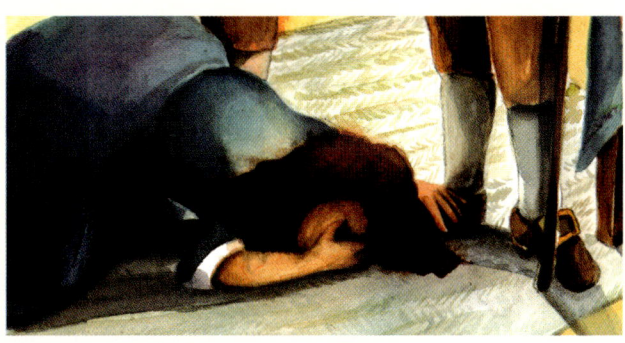

Cunégonde threw herself at his feet and bathed them with her tears, but the Baron was inflexible.

[Candide was very angry and thought the Baron was being ungrateful. He said,] 'I have taken you from the galleys and paid your ransom, and I have paid your sister's too. I found her washing dishes, and she's as ugly as a witch. Yet when I have the decency to make her my wife, you still pretend to raise objections. I should kill you again, if my anger got the better of me.'

'You can kill me again, if you like,' said the Baron, 'but while I live, you shall never marry my sister.'"

Although Cunégonde wanted to marry Candide, the baron refused because Candide was not of noble birth.

A Worldly Writer

Voltaire was French, but he spent half his life outside France—in England, the Netherlands, and in present-day Germany and Switzerland. He helped make great writers and thinkers, such as William Shakespeare, John Locke, and Isaac Newton, famous outside of England. He was a passionate writer who hated intolerance, superstition, and **tyranny**. Voltaire wrote almost until he took his last breath at the age of 83 in 1778. A few days before his death, he said, "I am ill, I am suffering from head to foot. Only my heart is sound, and this is no good for anything." He left an impressive literary legacy, including more than 21,000 letters and many essays and books. His ideas have had far-reaching effects and influenced people throughout the world. Voltaire's work continues to be read even today because his writing is filled with wit, and his stories are gracefully told and inventive. Perhaps most importantly, Voltaire's writing continues to make people think.

> **tyranny**: absolute power, especially when it is exercised in an unjust or cruel way

Quick Quiz

1. Why was Voltaire forced to leave Paris?
2. Why didn't the baron want Candide to marry his sister?
3. Why do you think *Candide* was a popular book during the Enlightenment?
4. How does the excerpt from *Candide* help you learn about the culture and history of Europe during the Enlightenment? How does it help you learn about class distinctions at this time?

Activities

After you have read one or more of the chapters in this book, you can play the following games and activities to make history come alive! You can do these on your own or with friends and family members.

PORTRAITS – Choose one of the people you read about in this book. Draw an outline of the person's profile. Inside the profile, write biographical information about the person, including when he or she lived and why he or she is remembered.

ALIKE OR DIFFERENT – Choose one of the people you read about in this book. Then think about how that person's life and the time in which that person lived is alike or different from your life today. Write this information on a Venn diagram. Analyze how the two eras are alike and different, as well as how your life is alike and different from the historical figure you chose.

A LETTER TO A FRIEND – The people who lived in the past were real people. Some enjoyed many advantages, but also encountered hardships and obstacles. Choose one of the people you read about in this book. Then write a letter to a friend that starts, "I met a remarkable writer today. Let me tell you about …" In your letter, be sure to tell what you admired about the writer, how the person's writing reflected ideas and values that the writer thought were important, advantages the person enjoyed, obstacles the person overcame, and words you would use to describe the person's character.

POETIC LICENSE – Choose one of the people you read about in this book. Write a poem about the writer on a piece of paper that is decorated with a symbol of "writing"—for example, you could place a pen or quill pen in one corner of the page. Follow the pattern below:

- Line 1: The person's name
- Line 2: One word to describe the person
- Line 3: Two words to describe the person
- Line 4: Three words to describe the person
- Line 5: The person's name

POSTER ART – Choose one of the people you read about in this book. Then create a "moment in time" poster showing one day in the person's life.

A PERSON TO REMEMBER – Choose one of the people you read about in this book. Then prepare a one-page report entitled, "A Person to Remember." Be sure to include the following information in your report:

Personal Information (year born, family, education, social class)
Description (how the person looked)
Character Traits (qualities the person possessed)
Achievements (what the person accomplished)
Descriptive Words (words you would use to describe the person)
Your Opinion (your opinion of the person)

CROSSWORD PUZZLER – Choose one or more of the people you read about in this book and create a crossword puzzle using words associated with the person or people. Here's an example!

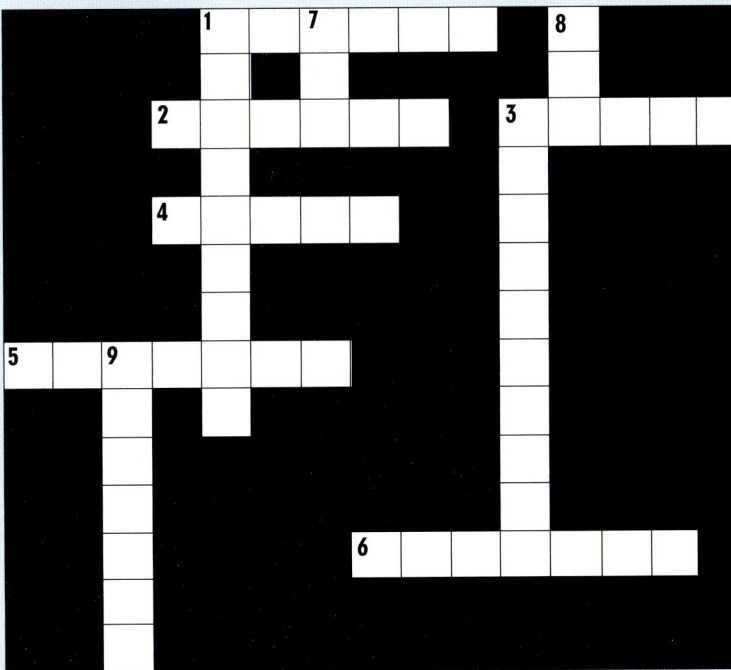

ACROSS
1. Dante wrote *The Divine* _____.
2. The main character in Lady Murasaki's novel was a _____.
3. Las Casas spoke out on behalf of the Indians of the New _____.
4. Place where Lady Murasaki's novel was set.
5. Shakespeare wrote plays and _____.
6. The ones who captured the Muslim historian and took him to the pope.

DOWN
1. The author of *Don Quixote de la Mancha*.
3. Europeans were very interested in knowing more about this part of the second largest continent.
7. Las Casas portrayed the Spanish conquistadors as _____ who were doing an injustice to the Indians.
8. _____ Africanus
9. One of William Shakespeare's plays is called *Much Ado about* _____.

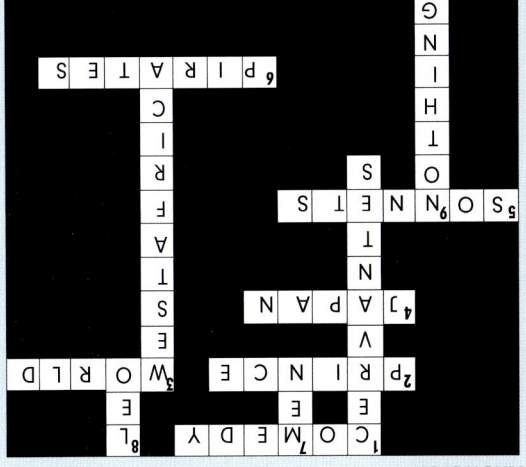
Answers:

71

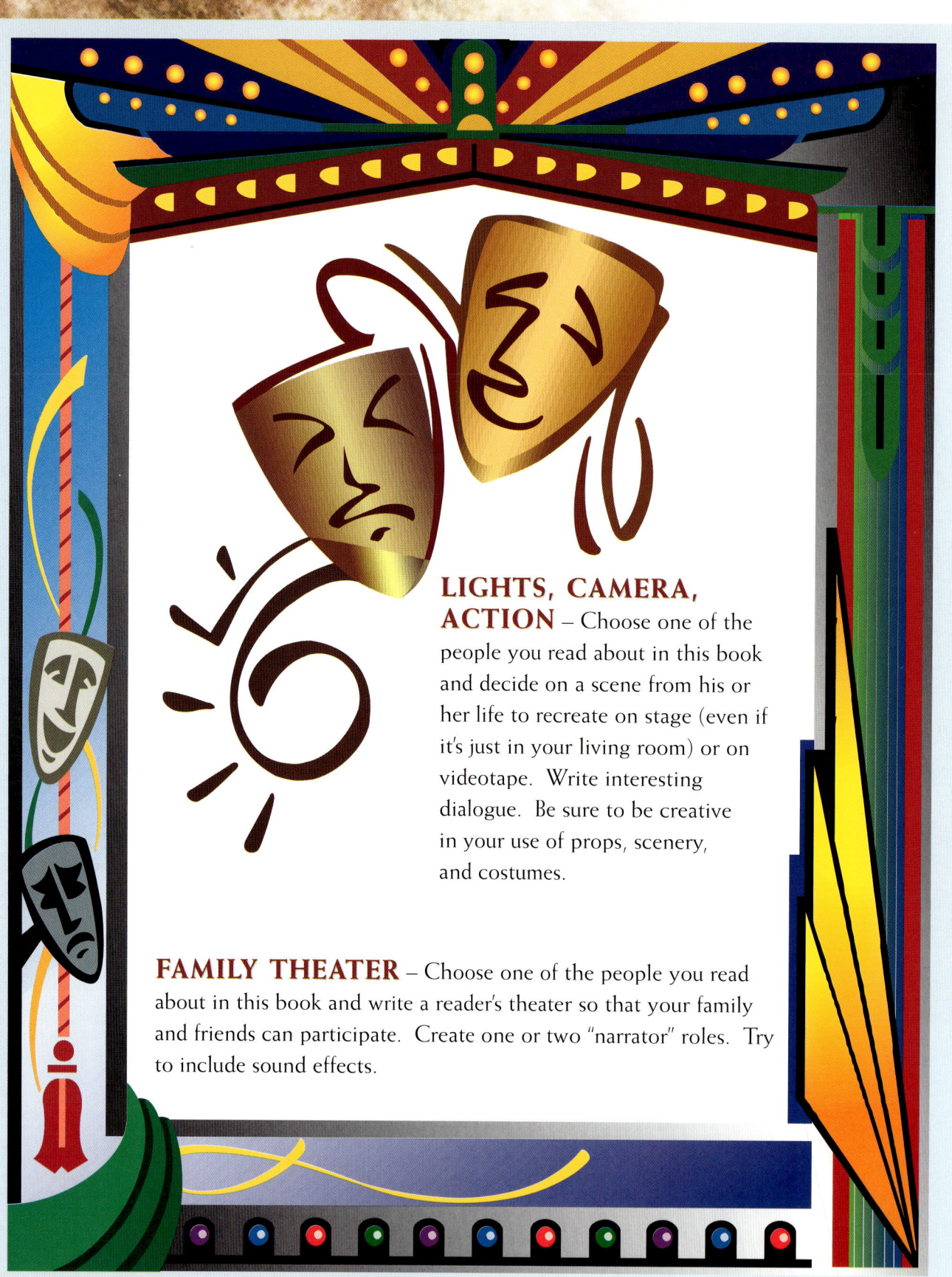

LIGHTS, CAMERA, ACTION – Choose one of the people you read about in this book and decide on a scene from his or her life to recreate on stage (even if it's just in your living room) or on videotape. Write interesting dialogue. Be sure to be creative in your use of props, scenery, and costumes.

FAMILY THEATER – Choose one of the people you read about in this book and write a reader's theater so that your family and friends can participate. Create one or two "narrator" roles. Try to include sound effects.

Test Your Knowledge!

PICK THE RIGHT ANSWER! (1 POINT EACH)

1. Throughout history, people have used the written word to _____.
    a. Describe events and convey emotions
    b. Influence opinions and free the imaginations of their readers
    c. All of the above

2. Which of the following people wrote mostly nonfiction work?
    a. Bartolomé de las Casas
    b. Miguel Cervantes
    c. William Shakespeare

3. Who wrote the world's first known novel?
    a. Leo Africanus
    b. Lady Murasaki
    c. Madame du Châtelet

4. Who wrote satirical stories to fight against intolerance and injustice?
    a. Voltaire
    b. Dante Aligheri
    c. Miguel Cervantes

WHO AM I? (1 POINT EACH)

5. I was given the title "Defender of the Indians" by the king of Spain and spent most of my life trying to improve the lives of Indians under Spanish rule.

    Who am I? _____

6. I wrote a story of my imaginary journey through the afterlife. Some people consider this story the greatest piece of literature of all time.

    Who am I? _____

MAKE A MATCH (1 POINT EACH)

7. aristocracy
8. Buddhism
9. Muslim
10. Renaissance
11. ransom
12. chivalry
13. sonnet
14. playwright
15. philosophe

a. a belief system
b. the nobility
c. the period in European history from about 1350-1600
d. how a knight must act—with respect for the church, pity for the poor, bravery, and courtesy
e. any of the leading philosophical, political, and social writers of the French Enlightenment
f. a person who writes plays
g. a payment made to release a hostage
h. a kind of poem
i. a person who follows the religion of Islam

Go to www.ballard-tighe.com/readingbookactivities for more activities and ways to test your knowledge!

WHAT'S YOUR SCORE?

14-15 points – TOP SCORE!   12-13 points – Good   10-11 points – Fair
Fewer than nine points? Read the book again!

Answers: 1c, 2a, 3b, 4a; 5-Bartolomé de las Casas, 6-Dante Aligheri; 7b, 8a, 9i, 10c, 11g, 12d, 13h, 14f, 15e

Glossary

agitation: (a-ji-TAY-shun) *n.* A state of being extremely upset or disturbed.
ambassador: (am-BAS-uh-dur) *n.* A person of high status who represents one government to another.
apprentice: (uh-PREN-tis) *n.* A beginning learner of a job.
arbitrary: (ahr-buh-TRAYR-ee) *adj.* Based on or subject to individual judgment.
attendant: (uh-TEN-dunt) *n.* A person who waits on or helps another.
balcony: (BAL-kuh-nee) *n.* A platform that sticks out of the wall of a building and is surrounded by a railing.
baptize: (BAP-tiyz) *v.* To dip in water or sprinkle with water; some people baptize their babies to make them a part of the Christian Church and give them a new Christian name.
baron: (BER-un) *n.* A nobleman.
Buddhism: (BOO-diz-um) *n.* A belief system that emphasizes freedom from wanting worldly possessions or power.
calligraphy: (kuh-LIG-ruh-fee) *n.* The art of fine handwriting.
cavern: (CA-vurn) *n.* A large cave or hollow area.

chivalry: (SHIV-uhl-ree) *n.* How a knight must act—with respect for the church, pity for the poor, bravery, and courtesy.
concubine: (KAHNG-kyuh-biyn) *n.* A woman who lives with and is supported by a man, but who is not his wife; mistress.
convent: (KAHN-vent) *n.* A place where a community of nuns lives.
conversion: (kuhn-VUR-zhun) *n.* The act of changing to a new religion, faith, or belief.
convey: (kuhn-VAY) *v.* To communicate or make known.
destitute: (DES-ti-toot) *adj.* Lacking.
discrimination: (di-skrim-uh-NAY-shun) *n.* Treatment based on class, race, or other category.
ducat: (DUHK-ut) *n.* Any of various gold coins formerly used in European countries.
embark: (em-BAHRK) *v.* To begin.
enmity: (EN-mi-tee) *n.* The feelings of an enemy; hostility.
etiquette: (ET-i-ket) *n.* A code of behavior and courtesy.
exile: (eg-ZIYL) *n.* Forced removal from one's native country.
favored: (FAY-vurd) *adj.* Privileged or indulged; treated specially.
foolish: (FOO-lish) *adj.* Silly; lacking good judgment or common sense.
fortuitous conjunction: (fohr-TOO-uh-tus kuhn-JUHNK-shun) *n.* Happy coincidence.
Good Friday: (gud FRIY-day) *n.* The Friday before Easter.
heir apparent: (ayr uh-PAYR-uhnt) *n.* A person who is believed to be entitled to receive an estate, title, or office after someone dies.
Holy Roman Empire: (HOH-lee ROH-mun EM-piyr) *n.* An empire, consisting largely of Germanic states in central and western Europe, established in 962 and ending in 1806.
humanity: (hyoo-MAN-i-tee) *n.* The human race.
immersed: (im-MURST) *v.* Deeply involved.
impart: (im-PAHRT) *v.* To teach.

PARTS OF SPEECH KEY

n. — **noun; a noun is a word that names a person, place, thing, or quality**
Examples: attendant, New World, mosque, chivalry

adj. — **adjective; an adjective is a word that describes, limits, qualifies, or specifies a person, place, thing, quality, or act**
Examples: favored, temperate, secular, destitute

v. — **verb; a verb is a word that expresses action, occurrence, or existence**
Examples: baptize, embark, convey

infatuation: (in-fa-choo-AY-shun) *n.* An intense, temporary love.
insolence: (IN-suh-luns) *n.* Arrogance; insulting manner or speech.
Islam: (IZ-lahm) *n.* A religion based on the teachings of the prophet Muhammad.
Jesuit: (JEZ-oo-it) *n.* A member of the Society of Jesus.
molest: (moh-LEST) *v.* To annoy or bother.
mosque: (mahsk) *n.* A Muslim place of worship.
Muslim: (MUZ-lum) *n.* A follower of Islam.
Negro: (NEE-groh) *n.* A person with dark skin from Africa; now considered to be an insulting term.
New World: (noo wurld) *n.* The term once used to describe North and South America.
pilgrim: (PIL-grum) *n.* A religious person who journeys to a sacred place.
plunder: (PLUN-dur) *v.* To rob or steal goods, especially in time of war.
pore: (pohr) *v.* To read or study carefully.
ransom: (RAN-sum) *n.* A payment made to release a hostage.
ravenous: (RA-vuh-nus) *adj.* Extremely hungry.
robust constitution: (roh-BUHST kahn-sti-TOO-shun) *n.* Healthy body.
Roman Catholic Church: (ROH-mun CATH-lik church) *n.* The Christian Church split into two churches in 1054; the Christian Church in the western part of the Roman Empire became known as the "Roman Catholic Church."
salvation: (sal-VAY-shun) *n.* Saving of the soul from sin and its consequences; the state of being saved.
satirical: (suh-TIR-i-kul) *adj.* Witty and mocking.
serf: (surf) *n.* A peasant worker who must work for a landowner and who may not quit or leave the land without permission.
slaughter: (SLAW-tur) *v.* To kill.
temperate: (TEM-pur-it) *adj.* Moderate.
tillable: (TIL-uh-bul) *adj.* Able to be plowed and used for agriculture.
torment: (TOHR-ment) *n.* Pain.

tyranny: (TEER-uh-nee) *n.* Absolute power, especially when it is exercised in an unjust or cruel way.
vie: (viy) *v.* To compete.
wares: (wayrs) *n.* Goods; articles for sale.

VOWEL PRONUNCIATION KEY

SYMBOL	KEY WORDS
a	ant, man
ay	cake, May
ah	clock, arm
aw	salt, ball
ayr	hair, bear
e	neck, bed
ee	ear, key
i	chick, skin
iy	five, tiger
oh	coat, soda
oi	boy, coin
ohr	board, door
oo	blue, boot
ow	cow, owl
u	foot, wolf, bird, and the schwa sound used in final syllables followed by 'l', 'r', 's', 'm', 't', or 'n'
uh	bug, uncle, and other schwa sounds

The vowel pronunciation key is derived from the following three sources: *American Heritage Dictionary of the English Language*, 1981; *Oxford American Dictionary: Heald Colleges Edition*, 1982; *Webster's New World College Dictionary, Third Edition*, 1990.

Index

A.D. 6-7
Aeneid, The 22
Africa 26, 33
age of exploration (European) 34, 36, 38
Akiko (Empress) 10
Alvarado, Pedro de 38
aristocracy 5, 8, 12, 62, 73
Arouet, François-Marie (see "Voltaire")
As You Like It 48, 50, 58
Augustus (Emperor) 22
B.C. 6-7
B.C.E. 6
B.P. 6
Beatrice 22-23
Breteuil, Gabrielle Emile Le Tonnelier de (see "Châtelet, Madame du")
Buddhism 13, 73
c. 6
Caesar, Julius 53
calligraphy 10
Candide 5, 7, 60, 62, 66-67, 69
Candide 66-69
Casas, Bartolomé de las 4, 7, 34-39, 73
C.E. 6
Cervantes, Miguel 4, 7, 40-47, 73
Charles V (king of Spain) 34, 38
Châtelet, Madame du 64-65, 73
chivalry 44, 46, 73
Christian 22, 33-34, 39
Christian Church 20-22, 42
Christianity 37-38
Cicero 63
circa 6
Columbus, Christopher 36
comedies 53, 59
Convivio 20
Cortés, Hernando 38
couplet 51
Cunégonde 66-68
Dante (Alighieri) 5-6, 18-25, 73
Dante (the Pilgrim) 22
dating system 6
Defender of the Indians 34
Divine Comedy, The 5-6, 18-19, 21-22, 24-25
Don Quixote 45-47

Don Quixote de la Mancha 4, 7, 40, 42, 44-46
Elizabeth I (queen of England) 48, 54-55
encomienda system 37
Enlightenment 60-63, 65, 69
etiquette 10, 17
Florence (Italy) 5, 18, 20-22, 25, 43
Frederick the Great (of Prussia) 64
Gao 30-31, 33
Genji 11-14, 16-17
gold (West Africa) 30
Good Friday 24
Greek 62
Greeks (ancient) 42
Hamlet 48
Hathaway, Anne 51
Heian period 5, 8, 11, 13
histories 53, 59
History and Description of Africa, The 5, 7, 26-28, 32-33
History of the Indies 4, 36, 38
Holy Roman Empire 67
Horace 63
"In Defense of the Indians" 7, 34, 39
Inca empire 38
Inferno (hell) 21-22, 24
Islam 29
Japan 5, 8, 10-11, 13; (aristocracy) 8
Jesuit 63
Jonson, Ben 53
Juliet 53, 56-57
King's Men 53
Kyoto 8, 14
las Casas (see "Casas, Bartolomé de las")
Latin 20, 24-25, 62, 65
Leo Africanus 5, 7, 26-33, 73
Leo X (pope) 33
Locke, John 69
London 48, 50, 53
Mali (kingdom of) 29
Middle Ages 18, 21, 25, 46
Morison, Samuel Eliot 38
mosque 29
Much Ado about Nothing 48, 50, 59
Muhammad, Askia 29
Muhammad, Hassan Ibn (see

"Leo Africanus")
Murasaki (Lady) 5-6, 8-17, 73
Muslim 29, 44, 73
New World 36-37
Newton, Isaac 65, 69
Niani 29
novel 5, 8-10, 12-13
Othello 48
Ovid 63
Paradiso (heaven) 21-22, 24
Paris 62-63, 65, 69
parody 44, 47
philosophe 60, 73
Pizarro, Francisco 38
playwright 48-49, 73
Purgatorio (purgatory) 21-22, 24
ransom 33, 44
Ravenna 20-21
Renaissance 42-44, 47, 50
Roman Catholic Church 21, 33, 63, 66
Roman Empire 18
Romans (ancient) 42, 53, 63
Romeo 48, 53, 56-57
Romeo and Juliet 7, 48, 53, 56-57
Sahara desert 28-29
salvation (Christian) 21
Shakespeare, William 5, 7, 48-59, 69, 73
Shikibu, Lady Murasaki (see "Murasaki [Lady]")
Songhai (kingdom of) 29
sonnet 5, 50-52, 73
stanza 51
Stratford-upon-Avon 50-51, 59
Tale of Genji, The 5-6, 8, 10-13, 16-17
terza rima 24
Timbuktu 29-30
time line 6-8, 18, 26, 34, 40, 48, 60
tragedies 53, 59
tyranny 69
United States of America 60
Venice 21
Virgil 22, 63
Vita Nuova 20
Voltaire 5, 7, 60-69, 73
West Africa 5, 26-30, 33

Skills Index/Credits

SKILLS INDEX

CONTENT LINKS
Religion 21-25, 29 , 33-34, 37-38, 63, 66
Economics 28-31, 37
Geography 4-8, 11, 18, 20-21, 26, 28-29, 34, 36, 40, 42, 48, 50, 60, 62
Government 20-21, 29-31, 34, 37-38, 60
History 6-79
Language Arts/Literature 6-79
Science 65, 69
Visual/Performing Arts, including art, architecture, and music 33, 48, 51, 53-59, 70-72

CHRONOLOGICAL AND SPATIAL THINKING
Understand key events and people of the historical era they are studying, both in a chronological sequence and within a spatial context. 4-8, 11, 18, 21, 26, 28, 34, 36, 40, 42, 48, 50, 60, 62
Identify how the present is connected to the past, identifying both similarities and differences between the two, and how some things change over time and some things stay the same. 4, 6-8, 11, 13, 17-18, 22, 24-26, 28-29, 33-34, 37-39, 47-48, 53, 58-60, 69-70

LANGUAGE DEVELOPMENT
Develop vocabulary. 6, 10, 12-13, 16, 20-22, 24, 29-30, 33, 36-37, 39, 44, 46, 51, 57, 59, 63, 66-67, 69; context clues/develop vocabulary in context. 6, 9-12, 18-19, 22, 24, 28-29, 33-34, 37-38, 42, 44, 48, 51, 53, 59-60, 64-65
Comprehend figurative language/idioms. 7, 10, 13, 16-17, 18, 21-22, 24-25, 29-31, 33-34, 36-39, 42, 44, 46, 51-53, 57, 59-60, 63-64, 66-67, 69
Comprehend reading material. 7, 17, 25, 33, 38, 47, 59, 69-73
Think critically. 7, 17, 25, 33, 38, 47, 59, 69-73

RESEARCH, EVIDENCE, AND POINT OF VIEW
Read primary sources. 10, 16-17, 24-25, 29-31, 34, 38-39, 44, 46, 48, 52-53, 57, 60, 63-64, 66-67
Pose questions about events encountered in historical documents, eyewitness accounts, oral histories, letters, diaries, artifacts, photographs, maps, artwork, and architecture. 7, 17, 25, 33, 38, 47, 59, 69
Conduct research. 70-72, 78
Interpret and analyze historical artifacts and accounts; examine conclusions, cause/effect relationships, and historical processes. 7, 10, 16-17, 20-21, 24-25, 29-31, 33, 38-39, 44, 46-48, 50, 52-53, 57, 59-60, 63-64, 66-67, 69
Develop historical empathy. 17, 25, 33, 38, 47, 59, 69, 70-73

ACADEMIC STUDY SKILLS
Acquire information by reading various forms of literature and primary and secondary source materials. 6-79
Read and interpret maps, charts, and pictures. 4-9, 11-15, 18-19, 21, 23, 25-28, 30-36, 38-43, 45, 47-50, 54-56, 58, 60-62, 64, 67-68
Understand the specialized academic language used in academic discourse, particularly in the social sciences. 6, 8, 11-13, 18, 21-22, 26, 28-31, 33-34, 36-38, 42, 44, 46, 50-51, 53, 60-63, 66, 74-75
Organize and express ideas clearly in writing and in speaking. 70-72

PICTURE CREDITS

ILLUSTRATORS
Patricia DeWitt and Robin DeWitt 33
Fujiko Miller 30

PICTURE RESOURCES
D. Appleton & Company. 1885. *The Hundred Greatest Men.* 61
Dodd, Mead and Company. 1902. *History of the World.* 49
Library of Congress 13, 38, 45, 47, 54-55
Allison Mangrum 25, 43
North Wind Picture Archives 35, 39, 41
Photographically Yours, **Dita Marina Obert** 58 (pictured from left, Ramlah Frediani, Erika Ceporius Miller, George Brunk)
Colored by Ronaldo Benaraw 49
Colored by Fred Sherman 12, 35, 38, 41, 45, 47, 54-55, 61

TEXT CREDITS

16-17 From *The Tale of Genji* by Lady Murasaki, translated with a foreword by Arthur Waley. The Modern Library, 1960. **24-25** From Dante Alighieri, *The Divine Comedy*, translated by Seth Zimmerman, *Willow Springs, Spoon River Poetry Review, Metamorphoses*. Proceedings of the American Translator's Association, 1993. **29**, **30-31** From Basil Davidson, *African Kingdoms*. Time Life, 1966. **38, 39** From Don Fray Bartolomé de las Casas's *In Defense of the Indians*, translated and edited by Stafford Pool, C. M. Northern Illinois University Press, 1974. **38** From Samuel Eliot Morison, *Admiral of the Ocean Sea*. Little, Brown, 1942. **44, 46** From Miguel de Cervantes, *Don Quixote*, translated by Samuel Putnam. Viking Press, 1949. **57** From William Shakespeare, *Romeo and Juliet*, edited by J. A. Bryant, Jr., New American Library, 1964. **60** From John Butt in Voltaire. *Candide*. Penguin Books, 1947. **62-63** From Theodore Besterman. *Voltaire*. Chicago Press, 1976. **66-67** From John Butt in Voltaire. *Candide*. Penguin Books, 1947.

Find Out More!

FIND MORE RESOURCES on our web site www.ballard-tighe.com/readingbookactivities

DANTE ALIGHERI:
Tusiani, Joseph. *Dante's Divine Comedy: As Told for Young People*. Brooklyn, NY: Legas, 2001. This book introduces young readers to Dante's masterpiece of literature. Nonfiction.

BARTOLOMÉ DE LAS CASAS:
Millar, Heather. *Spain in the Age of Exploration* (Cultures of the Past series). Tarrytown, NY: Marshall Cavendish, 1999. This easy-to-read book presents information about Spain's exploration in the New World, including the hardships explorers faced and their interactions with the native peoples. Good color illustrations. Nonfiction.

MIGUEL CERVANTES:
Goldberg, Jake. *Miguel de Cervantes*. New York: Chelsea House Publishers, 1993. This biography reveals the life of the Spanish writer who wrote the novel *Don Quixote*. Lots of black-and-white pictures and a chronology of events. Nonfiction.

Harrison, Michael. *Don Quixote* (Oxford Illustrated Classics). New York: Oxford University Press, 1999. This book focuses on several episodes in Cervantes's novel. Beautiful illustrations. Fiction, with a critical note at the end that provides a general context for the story.

WILLIAM SHAKESPEARE:
Aliki. *William Shakespeare & the Globe*. New York: HarperCollins, 1999. This is a beautifully written and illustrated work. Aliki combines literature, history, and art in this carefully researched and lovingly created book about Shakespeare and the theater he created. Includes a listing of his works, a chronology of his life, and some of the 2,000 words and expressions he created. Notable Trade Books in the Field of Social Studies. Nonfiction.

Blackwood, Gary L. *The Shakespeare Stealer*. New York: Dutton Books, 1998. This novel is set in England during Shakespeare's time. A young orphan is sent to copy down a play and has many experiences and adventures in the world of the Globe Theater. A Notable Social Studies Trade Book for Young People. Fiction.

Cooper, Susan. *King of Shadows*. New York: Aladdin Paperbacks, 2001. This novel finds Nat Field on his way to London to perform in a play at the reconstructed Globe Theater. However, he is switched in time with another Nat Field living in Shakespeare's day. Lots of adventures confront him! Fiction.

Lamb, Charles and Mary Lamb. *Tales from Shakespeare*. New York: Random House, 1999. This book will introduce you to 20 Shakespearean plays. Most of the stories are told in narrative form, but original language and dialogue from the plays are also included. Nonfiction.

Langley, Andrew. *Shakespeare's Theatre*. New York: Oxford University Press, 1999. *Shakespeare's Theatre* is the story of two theaters: the original Globe on the bank of the Thames River in London, opened in 1599, and its modern reconstructed twin, built in almost exactly the same spot and opened nearly 400 years later. Beautiful watercolor paintings! Nonfiction.

VOLTAIRE:
Dunn, John M. *The Enlightenment* (World History series). San Diego, CA: Lucent Books, 1990. This book provides a good general overview of the people and ideas of the Enlightenment. Nonfiction.

Acknowledgments

any people contributed their knowledge, talents, and enthusiasm to this book. We are indebted to a remarkable editorial staff, especially Allison Mangrum, and including Heera Kang, Kristin Belsher, and Patrice Gotsch. We also are indebted to Liliana Cartelli, the talented art director of the Explore the Ages series. She brought our ideas about pairing text and visuals to life and the result is more beautiful than we thought possible. We are grateful for helpful comments and suggestions on earlier drafts of this work by Dr. Diane L. Brooks, Dr. Cheryl Riggs, and David Vigilante. This book is dedicated to Georgia Stathis, a high school English teacher who inspired generations of fledgling writers.

Roberta Stathis & Gregory Blanch

Dr. Stathis is an educator, writer, and editor. Dr. Blanch is on the faculty at New Mexico State University. They are co-authors of People and Stories in World History: A Historical Anthology *(Ballard & Tighe, 2003) and other books in the Explore the Ages series—* Leaders Who Changed the World, Renaissance Artists Who Inspired the World, *and* Women Who Ruled *(Ballard & Tighe, 2004).*